LIFE'S GREATEST TREASURE

LIFE'S GREATEST TREASURE

BEAUTIFUL WRITINGS

ABOUT CHILDREN

SELECTED BY MARIANNE WILSON

AND PETER SEYMOUR

ILLUSTRATED BY FRANCES HOOK

 HALLMARK CROWN EDITIONS

CONTENTS

A CHILD IS BORN

WELCOME

The room you have in my heart is new,
I've made it especially nice for you!

I've freshened it with a sun-warmed breeze
That I caught napping in southern seas.

I've swept the floor with a scented brush
That grew in the desert's enchanted hush.

I've walked by the lake where the lupins bloom—
With the peace I found I furnished your room.

The walls I adorned with wistful dreams
Of flaming dawns and twilit streams.

I caught the soft notes of a robin's song—
Its melody lingers all the day long.

I sought the glowworm's golden light
And set it to shine in your window at night.

Beside the slow embers of kindled content
Long thoughts will find encouragement.

My arms will welcome you—keep you warm,
My love will shelter you from the storm.

EMILY CAREY ALLEMAN

6

CARL SANDBURG: A NEWBORN BABY

A baby is God's opinion that life should go on. Never will a time come when the most marvelous recent invention is as marvelous as a newborn baby. The finest of our precision watches, the most supercolossal of our supercargo planes, don't compare with a newborn baby in the number and ingenuity of coils and springs, in the flow and change of chemical solutions, in timing devices and interrelated parts that are irreplaceable.

MONDAY'S CHILD

Monday's child is fair of face,
Tuesday's child is full of grace,
Wednesday's child is full of woe,
Thursday's child has far to go,
Friday's child is loving and giving,
Saturday's child works hard for its living,
And a child that's born on the Sabbath day
Is fair and wise and good and gay.

ANONYMOUS

LOVE

I love these little people;
and it is not a slight thing
when they, who are so fresh
from God, love us.

CHARLES DICKENS

NORMAN VINCENT PEALE:
A WONDERFUL CREATION

What greater happiness can come to a family than the
arrival of a baby! Surely it is a sign that God has blessed
the marriage. A baby is God's masterpiece—a wonderful creation of His infinite mind. He has said, "Suffer
little children, and forbid them not, to come unto me:
for of such is the kingdom of heaven. . . ." No baby can
ever be far from the throne of God, the Source of all
life, of all creation.

WHERE DID YOU COME FROM, BABY DEAR?

Where did you come from, baby dear?
Out of the everywhere into the here.
Where did you get those eyes so blue?
Out of the sky as I came through.
What makes the light in them sparkle and spin?
Some of the starry spikes left in.
What makes your cheek like a warm white rose?
I saw something better than anyone knows.
Whence that three-cornered smile of bliss?
Three angels gave me at once a kiss.
Where did you get those arms and hands?
Love made itself into bonds and bands.
Feet, where did you come, you darling things?
From the same box as the cherubs' wings.
How did they all just come to be you?
God thought about me, and so I grew.
But how did you come to us, you dear?
God thought about you, and so I am here.

GEORGE MAC DONALD

LEO TOLSTOY: THE CRY OF LIFE
from Anna Karenina

And suddenly, from the mysterious and awful far away world in which he had been living for the last twenty-two hours, Levin felt himself all in an instant borne back to the old every-day world, glorified though now, by such a radiance of happiness that he could not bear it. The strained chords snapped, sobs and tears of joy which he had never foreseen rose up with such violence that his whole body shook, that for long they prevented him from speaking.

Falling on his knees before the bed, he held his wife's hand before his lips and kissed it, and that hand, with a weak movement of the fingers, responded to his kiss. And meanwhile, there at the foot of the bed, in the deft hands of Lizaveta Petrovna, like a flickering light in a lamp, lay the life of a human creature, which had never existed before, and which would now with the same right, with the same importance to itself, live and create in its own image.

"Alive! alive! And a boy too! Set your mind at rest!" he heard Lizaveta Petrovna saying, as she slapped the baby's back with a shaking hand.

"Mamma, is it true?" said Kitty's voice.

The princess's sobs were all the answer she could make. And in the midst of the silence there came an unmistakable reply to the mother's question, a voice quite unlike the subdued voices speaking in the room. It was the bold, clamorous, self-assertive squall of the new human being, who had so incomprehensibly appeared.

BABY'S EYES

In a baby's eyes,
The wonder of creation
Shines; the miracle
Of new life fresh from heaven,
Of a new soul God has blessed.

KATHERINE DAVIS

13

KATE DOUGLAS WIGGIN:
SOMEWHERE THE CHILD

Among the thousands of tiny things growing up all over the land, some of them under my very wing—watched and tended, unwatched and untended, loved, unloved, protected from danger, thrust into temptation—among them somewhere is the child who will write the novel that will stir men's hearts to nobler issues and incite them to better deeds.

There is the child who will paint the greatest picture or carve the greatest statue of the age; another who will deliver his country in an hour of peril; another who will give his life for a great principle; and another, born more of the spirit than of the flesh, who will live continually on the heights of moral being, and dying, draw men after him.

It may be that I shall preserve one of these children to the race. It is a peg big enough on which to hang a hope, for every child born into the world is a new incarnate thought of God, an ever fresh and radiant possibility.

A BABY'S HANDS

A baby's hands, like rosebuds furled,
    Where yet no leaf expands,
Ope if you touch, though close upcurled —
    A baby's hands.

Then, even as warriors grip their brands
    When battle's bolt is hurled,
They close, clenched hard like tightening
       bands.

No rosebuds yet by dawn impearled
    Match, even in loveliest lands;
The sweetest flowers in all the world—
    A baby's hands.
ALGERNON CHARLES SWINBURNE

CHILDHOOD VISIONS

RACHEL CARSON: A SENSE OF WONDER

A child's world is fresh and new and beautiful, full of wonder and excitement. It is our misfortune that for most of us that clear-eyed vision, that true instinct for what is beautiful and awe-inspiring, is dimmed and even lost before we reach adulthood.

If I had influence with the good fairy who is supposed to preside over the christening of all children, I should ask that her gift to each child in the world be a sense of wonder so indestructible that it would last throughout life, as an unfailing antidote against the boredom and disenchantment of later years, the sterile preoccupation with things that are artificial, the alienation from the sources of our strength.

If a child is to keep alive his inborn sense of wonder without any such gift from the fairies, he needs the companionship of at least one adult who can share it, rediscovering with him the joy, excitement and mystery of the world we live in.

OF GIANTS AND CASTLES

Babies do not want to hear about babies;
they like to be told of giants and castles,
and of somewhat which can stretch
and stimulate their little minds.

SAMUEL JOHNSON

WHO HAS SEEN THE WIND?

Who has seen the wind?
Neither I nor you:
But when the leaves hang trembling,
The wind is passing through.

Who has seen the wind?
Neither you nor I:
But when the trees bow down their heads,
The wind is passing by.

CHRISTINA ROSSETTI

TO BE A CHILD

Doomed as absurd adults, we can forget
That stories run through children's heads, the way
Young children run all through a summer day,
Hot in the blazing of the alphabet.
We watch her reading there, wearing her wild,
Utterly-given-up, ravenous look.
But see! It is as if a breathing book
Has picked her up and reads the living child.

This is to be a child: To heighten
Each thing you handle, to be shyer
Than rabbit in wide field, to frighten
Deep dark that scared you, to fly higher
Than kite or hunting hawk, to brighten
Daylight, because you are a fire.

PAUL ENGLE

THE MOON

I see the moon,
And the moon sees me;
God bless the moon,
And God bless me.
    Amen.
CELTIC CHILD'S SAYING

20

FOREIGN LANDS

Up into the cherry tree
Who should climb but little me?
I held the trunk with both my hands
And looked abroad on foreign lands.

I saw the next door garden lie,
Adorned with flowers, before my eye,
And many pleasant places more
That I had never seen before.

I saw the dimpling river pass
And be the sky's blue looking-glass;
The dusty roads go up and down
With people tramping in to town.

If I could find a higher tree
Farther and farther I should see,
To where the grown-up river slips
Into the sea among the ships.

To where the roads on either hand
Lead onward into fairy land,
Where all the children dine at five,
And all the playthings come alive.

ROBERT LOUIS STEVENSON

TELL ANY CHILD

Earth,
tell any child who runs you in the spring
    under the froth of buds,
dreams on you under the summer sky or in
    the emerald cave of hemlock,
who scuffs your autumn drifts
       of roadside color,
and flies with flying flakes across
       your breast—
Earth, tell any child
that you are his forever, that he is
the happy owner of a tilting world,
of blossoms by the bushel-basket, tons
of leaves, cloud-shadow-miles, sun, rain
       and snow.
Tell him, Earth,
that he has deed and title
to beauty by the acre
anywhere he breathes!

           FRANCES FROST

FRANCIS THOMPSON:
KNOW YOU WHAT IT IS TO BE A CHILD?

Know you what it is to be a child? It is to be something very different from the man of today. It is to have a spirit yet streaming from the waters of baptism, it is to believe in love, to believe in loveliness, to believe in belief. It is to be so little that the elves can reach to whisper in your ear. It is to turn pumpkins into coaches, and mice into horses, lowness into loftiness and nothing into everything—for each child has his fairy godmother in his own soul. It is to live in a nutshell and count yourself king of the infinite space; it is

To see the world in a grain of sand,

Heaven in a wild flower,

To hold infinity in the palm of your hand,

And Eternity in an hour.

WONDER OF LIFE

Children are the most wholesome part of the
human race, the sweetest, for they are freshest
from the hand of God.

   Whimsical, ingenious, mischievous, they fill the
world with joy and good humor. We adults live
a life of apprehension as to what they will think
of us; a life of defense against their terrifying energy;
a life of hard work to live up to their great
expectations. We put them to bed with a sense of
relief—and greet them in the morning with delight
and anticipation. We envy them the freshness
of adventure and the discovery of life.

   In all these ways, children add to the wonder of
being alive. In all these ways, they help to keep
us young.

                          HERBERT HOOVER

THE EYES OF A CHILD

A child's eyes, those clear wells of undefiled
thought—what on earth can be more beautiful?
Full of hope, love and curiosity, they meet your
own. In prayer, how earnest; in joy, how sparkling;
in sympathy, how tender! The man who never tried
the companionship of a little child has carelessly
passed by one of the great pleasures of life,
as one passes a rare flower without plucking it
or knowing its value.

CAROLINE NORTON

THE FIRST BABY

When the first baby laughed for the first time,
the laugh broke into a thousand pieces and they
all went skipping about, and that was the
beginning of fairies.

JAMES BARRIE

"G" AS IN "GIRL"

WHAT IS A GIRL?

A girl is a charming and wonderful being
In T-shirt or dress trimmed with lace,
A lover of dolls and little stray kittens—
A creature of beauty and grace.
A girl is a fountain of bubbling laughter,
With pigtails or gay, bouncing curls,
She loses her crayons and pennies and ribbons,
And loves to share secrets with girls.
She likes to play house with some other
      small "mothers"
Or run down the street jumping rope,
Or climb on your lap for that extra story,
Her heart full of undaunted hope,
She's a lover of tea parties, ice cream
      and candy,
Of paper dolls, mud pies, and pets,
Of sandpiles and roller skates, makeup
      and dancing,
And every new doll that she gets,
A girl is a mixture of imp and of angel,
Of wonder and sudden surprise,
With a woman's enchantment and magic
      and vision,
With stardust and faith in her eyes.

KATHERINE DAVIS

WHY GOD MADE LITTLE GIRLS

God made the world with its towering trees,
Majestic mountains and restless seas,
Then paused and said,
"It needs one more thing—
Someone to laugh and dance and sing,
To walk in the woods and gather flowers,
To commune with nature in quiet hours,"
So God created little girls
With laughing eyes and bouncing curls,
With joyful hearts and infectious smiles,
Enchanting ways and feminine wiles,
And when He'd completed the task He'd begun
He was pleased and proud of the job He'd done,
For the world, when seen through
      a little girl's eyes,
Greatly resembles Paradise.

BARBARA BURROW

AGE OF PERFECTION

"One" I thought a lovely age.
  "Two" seemed better still.
"Three!" Ah, that's life's golden stage,
  Rich with many a thrill!
Then, as many a gray-haired man,
  Foolish to the core,
Vowed there's nothing lovelier than
  Little girls of four.

"Four," the time of sparkling eyes,
  Twinkling with delight,
Everything a glad surprise,
  Life exactly right.
Romping all the hours away,
  "Time can have in store
Nothing lovelier," I'd say,
  "Than this age of four."

Now that year has come and gone,
  Never more to be,
Still the charms I look upon
  Glorious are to see.

Still those eyes with gladness glow,
  Still those charms survive!
All the radiance "four" could show
  Lovelier seems at five!

                    EDGAR A. GUEST

32

HEART'S CHILD

She is the sunrise, flaming bright,
A petal unfolding to the light.

The scarlet flash of a cardinal's wing,
The rippling music small brooks sing.

She is the freshness of morning dew,
The loveliness of the rainbow's hue.

The heaven-borne song of the nightingale,
The witchery of a fairy tale.

She is beauty's haunting refrain,
The shining silver of slanting rain.

She is a story just begun
Of love and laughter, heartbreak and fun!

EMILY CAREY ALLEMAN

OF A SMALL DAUGHTER
WALKING OUTDOORS

Easy, wind!   She is new
Go softly here!   To walking, so,
She is small   Wind, be kind
And very dear.   And gently blow

She is young   On her ruffled head,
And cannot say   On grass and clover.
Words to chase   Easy wind . . .
The wind away.   She'll tumble over!

FRANCES FROST

THE FUTURE

When I see the motherly airs of my little
daughters when playing with their puppets, I
cannot but flatter myself that their husbands
and children will be happy in the possession
of such wives and mothers.

JOSEPH ADDISON

AN EXQUISITE POEM

*A little girl-child! The very idea
is the most exquisite of poems!
a child-daughter—wherein it seems to me
that the spirit of all dews and flowers
and springs and tender sweet wonders
"strikes its being into bonds."*

SYDNEY DOBELL

NANCY

You are a rose, but set with sharpest spine;
You are a pretty bird that pecks at me;
You are a little squirrel on a tree,
Pelting me with the prickly fruit of the pine;
A diamond, torn from a crystal mine,
Not like that milky treasure of the sea,
A smooth, translucent pearl, but skillfully
Carved to cut, and faceted to shine.
If you are flame, it dances and burns blue;
If you are light, it pierces like a star
Intenser than a needlepoint of ice.
The dexterous touch that shaped the soul of you,
Mingled, to mix, and make you what you are,
Magic between the sugar and the spice.

ELINOR WYLIE

37

THOMAS JEFFERSON:
  TO A GRANDDAUGHTER

My Dear Ellen,

I have received your letter and am very happy to learn you have made such rapid progress in learning. When I left Monticello you could not read and now I find you can not only read but write also. I enclose you two little books as a mark of satisfaction, and if you continue to learn as fast you will become a learned lady and publish books yourself. I hope you will at the same time continue to be a very good girl, never getting angry with your playmates nor the servants, but always trying to be more good humored and more generous tempered than they. If you find that one of them has been better tempered to you than you to them, you must blush, and be very much ashamed, and resolve not to let them excel you again. In this way you will make us all too fond of you, and I shall particularly think of nothing but what I can send you or carry you to show you how much I love you. . . . I have given this letter 20 kisses which it will deliver to you: half to yourself, and the other half you must give to Anne. Adieu my dear Ellen.

      (written to Eleanor Randolph, November 27, 1801)

SYDNEY SMITH: ADVICE TO A YOUNG GIRL

Lucy, Lucy, my dear child, don't tear your frock: tearing frocks is not of itself a proof of genius; but write as your mother writes, act as your mother acts; be frank, loyal, affectionate, simple, honest; and then integrity or laceration of frock is of little import.

And Lucy, dear child, mind your arithmetic. You know, in the first sum of yours I ever saw, there was a mistake. You had carried two (as a cab is licensed to do) and you ought, dear Lucy, to have carried but one. Is this a trifle? What would life be without arithmetic, but a scene of horrors . . . ? I now give you my parting advice. Don't marry anyone who has not a tolerable understanding and a thousand a year; and God bless you, dear child!

July 22, 1835

"B" AS IN "BOY"

WHAT IS A BOY?

A boy is a mischievous, magical creature,
An angel with mud on his face,
A daredevil climber of trees and of rafters,
Who loves any game, any place.
A boy is a keeper of frogs and of beetles,
Whose pockets are stuffed full of string,
An apple, a slingshot, some half-eaten candy
A knife and a new signet ring,
He is found camping out with adventuresome
      playmates,
Or making a rod and a reel,
Or swinging a bat in an old empty lot,
But can seldom be found for a meal,
He's a bubble gum fan and a comic book reader,
Likes westerns and space ships and noise,
Bicycles, screwdrivers, roller skates,
      bottles,
But most of all likes—other boys.
A boy is a craftsman, a builder, a dreamer,
Whose hopes are as wide as the world,
In the heart of a boy is the hope
      of the future,
A banner of courage unfurled!

KATHERINE DAVIS

MIDNIGHT ON THE GREAT WESTERN

In the third-class seat sat the journeying boy,
   And the roof-lamp's oily flame
Played down on his listless form and face,
Bewrapt past knowing to what he was going,
    Or whence he came.

In the band of his hat the journeying boy
   Had a ticket stuck; and a string
Around his neck bore the key of his box,
That twinkled gleams of the lamp's sad beams
    Like a living thing.

What past can be yours, O journeying boy
   Towards a world unknown,
Who calmly, as if indifferent quite
To all at stake, can undertake
    This plunge alone?

Knows your soul a sphere, O journeying boy,
   Our rude realms far above,
Whence with spacious vision you mark and mete
This region of sin that you find you in,
    But are not of?

THOMAS HARDY

OF BOYS AND DOGS

The coat of a dog makes a wonderful sponge
For the tears of an unhappy boy.
The neck of a dog is a fine thing to hug
When a small throat is choking with joy.

Courage is greater when faithfully backed
By a tail-wagging amateur sleuth.
Dogs seem to be indispensable rungs
Up the ladder to manhood from youth.

GEORGIA SYKES SULLIVAN

GIFTS FROM A SMALL BOY

His small hands overflowing with rainbow-tinted bloom,
He quietly, half-shyly, tiptoed to my room;
"These posies are for you," he said,
Then hurrying through the door,
Left me with more than flowering wreath,
So much—O so much—more!

KATHERINE EDELMAN

Build me a son, O Lord, who will be strong enough to know when he is weak, and brave enough to face himself when he is afraid; one who will be proud and unbending in honest defeat, and humble and gentle in victory.

Build me a son whose heart will be clear, whose goal will be high; a son who will master himself before he seeks to master other men; one who will learn to laugh, yet never forget how to weep; one who will reach into the future, yet never forget the past. And after all these things are his, add, I pray, enough of a sense of humor, so that he may always be serious, yet never take himself too seriously. Give him humility, so that he may always remember the simplicity of true greatness, the open mind of true wisdom, the meekness of true strength. Then I, his father, will dare to whisper, "I have not lived in vain."

HALF-PAST THREE

My friend has a yacht, a house by the sea,
But I have a boy who is half-past three.

I have no jewels, no satin gown,
But I have a boy who is butter-nut brown.

My friend has an orchid, my friend has a rose,
But I have a boy with a freckled nose.

O gull tell the waves that I have no yacht.
Wind, tell the wild forget-me-not

That I have no jewels, no shimmering gown,
No satin slippers, no pillows of down,

But I have a robin, a wind-swept hill,
A pocket of dreams, a heart to fill,

And I have a boy who is half-past three—
A little lad who looks like me.

EMILY CAREY ALLEMAN

WHY GOD MADE LITTLE BOYS

God made a world out of His dreams
Of majestic mountains, oceans and streams,
Prairies and plains, and wooded land,
Then paused and thought,
      "I need someone to stand
On top of the mountains, to conquer the seas,
Explore the plains, and climb the trees—
Someone to start out small and grow
Sturdy and strong like a tree," and so—
He created boys, full of spirit and fun,
To explore and conquer, to romp and run,
With dirty faces and bandaged shins,
With courageous hearts and boyish grins,
And when He'd completed the task He'd begun,
He surely said "That's a job well done."

PATRICIA WHITE

PEARL BUCK: 'I HAVE A SON'
from *The Good Earth*

The red candle was lit and she was lying neatly covered upon the bed. Beside her, wrapped in a pair of his old trousers, as the custom was in this part, lay his son.

He went up and for the moment there were no words in his mouth. His heart crowded up into his breast and he leaned over the child to look at it. It had a round wrinkled face that looked very dark and upon its head the hair was long and damp and black. It had ceased crying and lay with its eyes tightly shut.

He looked at his wife and she looked back at him. Her hair was still wet with her agony and her narrow eyes were sunken. Beyond this, she was as she always was. But to him she was touching, lying there. His heart rushed out to those two and he said, not knowing what else there was that could be said,

"Tomorrow I will go into the city and buy a pound of red sugar and stir it into boiling water for you to drink."

And then looking at the child again, this burst forth from him suddenly as though he had just thought of it, "We shall have to buy a good basketful of eggs and dye them all red for the village. Thus will everyone know I have a son!"

WEE LADDIE

Two dimpled hands,
Ten tiny toes,
One rosebud mouth,
One snubby nose.

A soft gurgling laugh,
An innocent smile,
A good healthy yell
Once in a while.

A pair of bright eyes,
Twin pools of blue,
Sunshine and showers
Reflecting through.

I'm lost in the wonder
Of life's greatest joy
As I gaze on the face
Of my wee sleeping boy.

MILLY WALTON

from THE BAREFOOT BOY

Blessings on thee, little man,
Barefoot boy, with cheek of tan!
With thy turned-up pantaloons,
And thy merry whistled tunes;
With thy red lip, redder still
Kissed by strawberries on the hill;
With the sunshine on thy face,
Through thy torn brim's jaunty grace;
From my heart I give thee joy —
I was once a barefoot boy!

JOHN GREENLEAF WHITTIER

51

THE JOYS OF PARENTHOOD

THERE IS A TIME

A child?
There is a time at the beginning
when your child is very close to you,
never going far from your side.

This is the time when, completely innocent,
a child asks only to love and to be loved.

This is the time
when a child reaches joyfully
toward a smile and a touch.

This is a time when a child goes naked.
And he asks you to put nothing on,
to be just what you really are.

Nothing can be hidden
from the soft eyes of a child.

Everything must be out in the open
between you two.

There comes a time of first looking,
of first wandering,
of stretching high,
searching,
sniffing,
and discovering the wonder of the world.

This is the time
when small fingers touch lightly,
delicately raising beauty to young lips.

This is the time for careful looking,
for happy surprise,
for reveling in the newness of things,
when all the world is fresh,
and its freshness brings only joy.

HUBERT BERMONT

A CHILD ASLEEP

How lovely he appears! his little cheeks
In their pure incarnation, vying with
The rose leaves strewn beneath them.
And his lips, too,
How beautifully parted! No; you shall not
Kiss him; at least not now; he will wake soon—
His hour of midday rest is nearly over.

GEORGE GORDON, LORD BYRON

MARGARET MEAD:
'TWO KINDS OF FEELING'

Often, as a mother bathes, feeds, and dresses her child, her face expresses two kinds of feeling that seem contradictory to the child and to the bystander. There is the look of unconditional devotion and blind pride in this, her child, and at the same time a look of anxious appraisal as she holds the infant away from her breast or watches the toddler's first stumbling steps and rocking gait.

For the child must go forth from the warmth and safety of its mother's care—first to take a few steps across the room, then to join playmates, and later to go to school, to work, to experience courtship and marriage, and to establish a new home. A boy must learn how different he is from his mother; he must learn that his life is turned outward to the world. A girl must learn, as she walks beside her mother, that she is both like her mother and a person in her own right. It is one of the basic complications of a mother's life that she must teach one thing to her sons and other things to her daughters.

Some peoples emphasize the mother's task more than the child's; they say that it is the mother, not the child, who is weaned. But all peoples, however differently they phrase the mystery of conception and provide for the care and safety of the mother and the child at birth, make provision—some well and others in a blundering way—for this double aspect of motherhood. All peoples build into their conception of the relationship of mother and child the care that must continue and the slowly awakening recognition that these are two persons—at birth, at physical weaning, at the child's first step, and at the child's first word that allows the child to call from a distance. And as the child lets go of its mother's hand, [it is] sure that it can return to be fed and rocked and comforted. . . .

On this unbroken continuity, on this ebb and flow of feeling between the child and the mothering woman, depends the child's sense of being a whole, continuing person—the same person today, yesterday, and tomorrow, the same person tired or rested, hungry or satiated, sleepy or wakeful, adventurous or quietly contented.

PETER MARSHALL: A FAMILY PRAYER

Lord Jesus, we would thank Thee that Thou hast blessed our home with the gift of young life, for we know that through our children Thou wouldst remind us of God.

We do resolve, by Thy help, to honor Thee in all our relationships—in our home, so that it may be Thy temple; in our hearts, where Thou dost love to dwell; in our place of business, that it may become an adventure in living our faith.

And now Lord, we place every member of our family in Thy care and keeping. Bless them every one. Be with us all throughout this day . . . . In Jesus' name. Amen.

SLEEPING CHILD

I like to tiptoe round her when she's lying
                    fast asleep
And straighten out the covers where she's kicked
                    them in a heap,
And when I find her sprawling kitty-corner
                    on the bed
I find it fun to set aright that lovely sleepy-head.
She's grown so very lively that she can't stay
                    still at all.
The moment that she drops asleep she starts right
                    in to crawl,
And sometimes, like a wooly dog, as comfy as
                    you please,
I've found her lost in dreamland with her head
                    between her knees.
Oh, I have tasks that weary me, and tasks
                    that I detest,
The mother's always calling me to work when
                    I would rest,
But straightening out a little girl who's sleeping
                    wrong-end to,
I'd call the happiest task on earth a father
                    has to do.

EDGAR A. GUEST

HOPE

A child, more than all other gifts
That earth can offer to declining man,
Brings hope with it, and forward looking thoughts.

WILLIAM WORDSWORTH

TO A BOY TWO DAYS OLD

Be strong, my son; stay ever out of debt;
depend not on your sire for livelihood;
have a good time; be merry and clever, and let
who will be good.

FRANKLIN PIERCE ADAMS

A LITTLE CHILD

A little child, a limber elf,
Singing, dancing to itself,
A fairy thing with red round cheeks
That always finds, and never seeks....

SAMUEL TAYLOR COLERIDGE

JAMES KELLER:
A PRAYER FOR NEW PARENTS

O Lord, give us the wisdom—
To deal with our children as You would,
To see in each of them Your Holy Image,
To develop in them a Christ-like love of
all men, not only a select few,
To nurture in them a divine desire to
"put in" and not simply "take out,"
To teach them to be "go-givers" rather
than "go-getters."
O God, in training these dear ones whom
Thou hast entrusted to our charge, help us—
To encourage rather than discourage them,
To discipline with kindness not softness,
To guide them intelligently, not blindly,
To coach, not scold; to nudge, not nag.
Dear Lord, above all, help us—
To use common sense in regard to their
future,
To let them go gladly when the time comes,
To let them lead their own lives while
following them with our love,
To pray always that they will be close to
Thee, not only for the few years of this life
but for the endless years of eternity.

RABINDRANATH TAGORE: THE GIFT

I want to give you something, my child, for we are drift-
ing in the stream of the world. Our lives will be carried
apart, and our love forgotten. But I am not so foolish as
to hope that I could buy your heart with gifts. Young is
your life, your path long, and you drink the love we
bring you at one draught and turn and run away from
us. You have your play and your playmates. What
harm is there if you have no time or thought for us?

We, indeed, have leisure enough in old age to count
the days that are past, to cherish in our hearts what our
hands have lost forever.

The river runs swift with a song, breaking through
all barriers. But the mountain stays and remembers,
and follows her with his love.

TO SMILE

To smile
Is to see fat puppies
Tumbling in the sun
Or children in a sprinkler,
Kaleidoscope of fun.

To smile
Is to cup a kitten
Gently in your hand,
Or watch small children with buckets,
Engrossed in sea and sand.

To smile
Is to see a duckling
Scamper through spring rain,
Or muse upon the magic
Of childhood joys again.

DORIS CHALMA BROCK

Set in Goudy light Old Style, a delicately styled
original alphabet drawn by the American designer
Frederic W. Goudy for the Monotype in 1905.
Printed on Hallmark Eggshell Book Paper.
Designed by William M. Gilmore.